BRUNO MUNARI   TH

Niall O'Sullivan

THE EQUILATERAL TRIANGLE

The illustrations and information contained in this book are only about equilateral triangles and not other triangles like right-angled triangles, isosceles triangles and scalene triangles in all their variations. Whereas a right-angled triangle can have different length sides and hence be different shapes, the equilateral triangle is the most stable form with its fixed structure of three equal sides and three equal angles. Its distinctive structure means we find it in lots of even complex structures and in many mineral and vegetable forms and structures found in nature, ranging from the clover to the oleander.

The equilateral triangle is one of the three basic forms, along with the circle and square. A full pattern of equilateral triangles touching on a surface creates a structured field in which endless other combinatorial forms may be constructed, as we can see in many Arab, Chinese, Persian and Japanese decorations. Many styles of decorative art are based around a triangular structure. A triangular (or tetrahedral) structure also gives the overall formal balance to lots of works of pure art. Nowadays, many constructions are based on a triangular structure and the modules deriving from it; we might, for example, mention the modulated constructions designed by Buckminster Fuller and a number of works of architecture by Wright and other young architects or classical constructors. An equilateral triangle can easily be found inside a circle by measuring its radius six times around the circumference and joining its three equidistant points by three lines. An equilateral triangle can be found inside a cube by joining the opposite ends of the three lines meeting at any apex. A cube has a tetrahedron inscribed inside it.

Understanding every aspect and formal-structural possibility of this simple, basic form is a great help to a designer. Due to static reasons, design-construction practicalities and economic factors connected with manufacture, transport and assembly, a modulated construction is now easier to design than the kind of visually striking-pictorial-sculptural construction that used to be built. The most popular structure in these cases is square-based, but it is also the blandest. On the other hand, triangular and tetrahedral structuring often produces more unexpected results, ideal, for example, for designing an exhibition facility which must really stand out in its setting.

In the field of technical-artistic education, experimentation with triangular forms and structures is common practice in design schools. A lot of the illustrations in this book are the result of experiments like this carried out in various schools.

Coherent forms may be constructed in model form, using sheets structured in the form of equilateral triangles, by cutting the sheet along the structural line and folding it according to the angle of the equilateral triangle.

One of the strangest traits of this kind of triangle is that, when drawn over a sphere covering one eighth of the space, it will always be an equilateral triangle with three right angles.

OLD TRADEMARK

One of the very oldest trademarks used for marking ceramic products.

ALVAR AALTO

Stoll construction around a fan-shaped juncture of prefabricated elements, 1954.

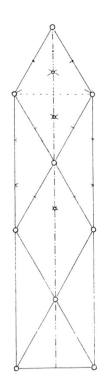

APOLLO OF TENEA AND EGYPTIAN STATUE

Statue of Apollo of Tenea and its harmonious structural scheme, the same as that used for Egyptian statues. Taken from a study by Ernst Mössel.

AŠŠUR

Sign for the deity Aššur in cuneiform writing.

LOW RELIEF

Decoration on a wooden wall with three-dimensional patterns linked to the triangular structure.

BOSCHIN

Tetrahedral structure composed of interlocking hexagons. The modular element is composed of three hexagons. The illustrations on the opposite page show examples of combination of these modules.

BANANA

The fruit's pulp is divided into three equal sectors.

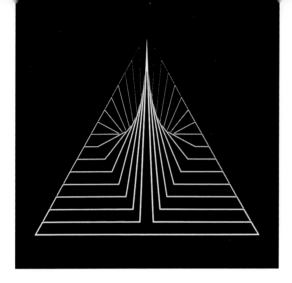

BERTOLIO

Architecture of a triangle, 1974.

BUDDHA

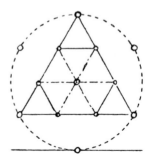

Statue of Buddha and its harmonious structural scheme.

BORROMINI

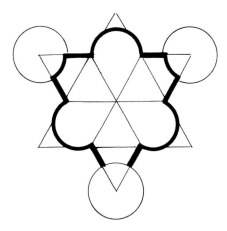

Geometric scheme of the plan of S. Ivo alla Sapienza in Rome, 1650.

COCONUT

The embryonic attachments of a coconut. The triangular vegetable structure can also be seen in the bottom part of the fruit.

CRYSTALS

Triangular figures in the attachment of silver crystals according to the 1-1-1 plane of Miller index. Micro-photograph.

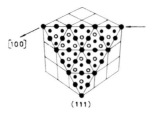

CUCUMBER

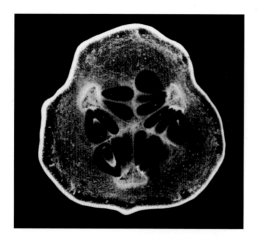

Section of the fruit showing the seeds arranged in triangular equilibrium.

STRUCTURED FIELD

Two-dimensional surface structured into equilateral triangles.

CALLIMITRA

Skeleton of the *Callimitra agnesae* radiolarian measuring approximately 15 millimetres in diameter.

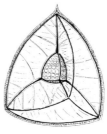

DONZELLI

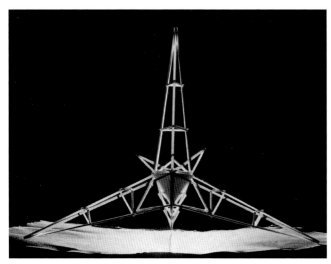

Model of a large luminous floating structure to be floated on the waters of Lake Como for a city festival.
Rinaldo Donzelli, 1963.

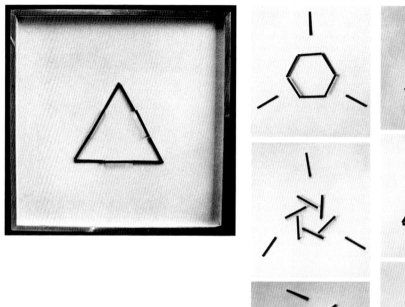

DADDA

Kinetic work driven by clockwork motors, Dario Dadda, 1972.
The sides of a triangle are divided into nine equal segments and each segment is attached at one of its ends to the pin of the minutes of battery-operated clock movement lasting one year. The segments then rotate with the imperceptible movement of the fingers of the clock and turn the basic starting form into lots of other forms, since each of the nine mechanisms manipulates the positions and times.

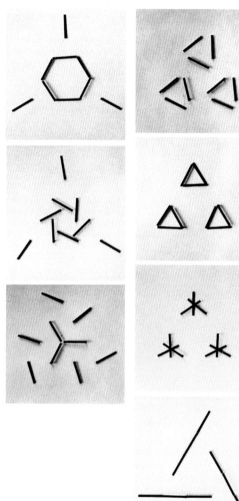

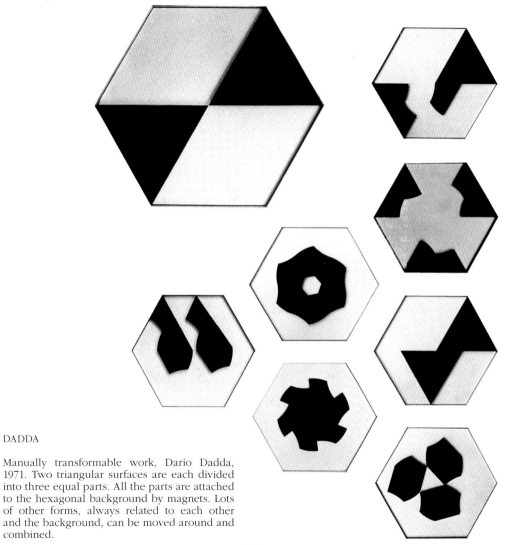

DADDA

Manually transformable work, Dario Dadda, 1971. Two triangular surfaces are each divided into three equal parts. All the parts are attached to the hexagonal background by magnets. Lots of other forms, always related to each other and the background, can be moved around and combined.

DELAUNAY

Black and yellow coloured drawing by Sonia Delaunay.

DECORATION

Decorative element drawn with a compass on a triangular base.

OPTICAL DEFORMATIONS

Experiment carried out by Franco Grignani into the deformation of a regular geometric image seen through pieces of glass moulded into different reliefs.

PHYLLOTAXIS

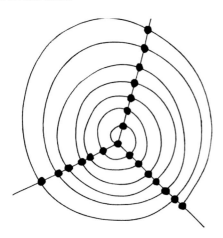

Trystic arrangement of the leaves of a plant along the stem.

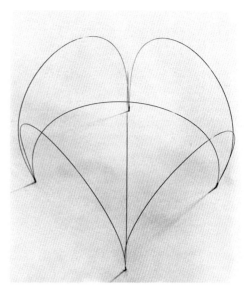

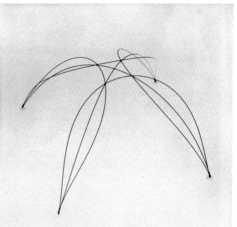

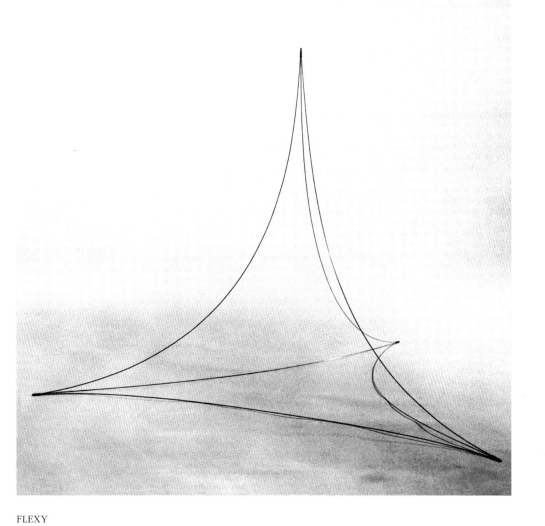

FLEXY

Limitless multiple of a flexible and transformable steel wire. Bruno Munari, 1968.

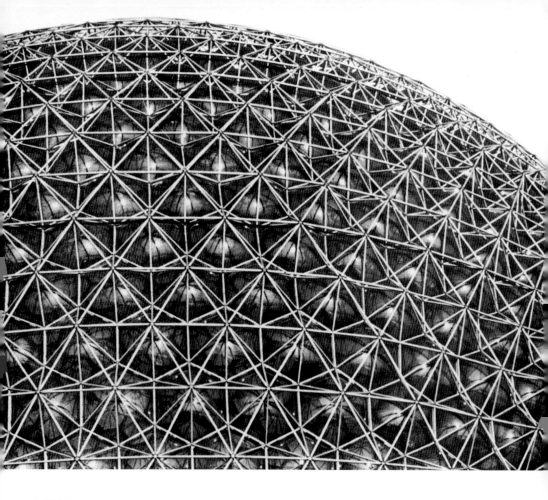

FULLER

Giant dome for the Montreal Expo. The entire structure is composed of a double triangular-based grid. Buckminster Fuller, 1967.

COHERENT FORMS

Forms derived from surfaces structured around equilateral triangles, cut along the structural lines and folded along the angle of the triangle. Exercise by students from the Carpenter Center, Harvard University, USA, 1967.

FORTRESS

Study of a triangular fortress. Giuliano da Sangallo (1445-1516) from the "Taccuino senese". Siena, City Library.

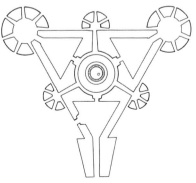

GAUDENZI

Tetrahedron sectioned over a fifth of its volume. The object, designed and constructed by Annamaria Gaudenzi out of transparent metacrylic, has two parts. Each part contains a proportional amount of distilled water. The two parts can be composed in various ways and the volume of water settles according to how the pieces are positioned, creating various compositions.

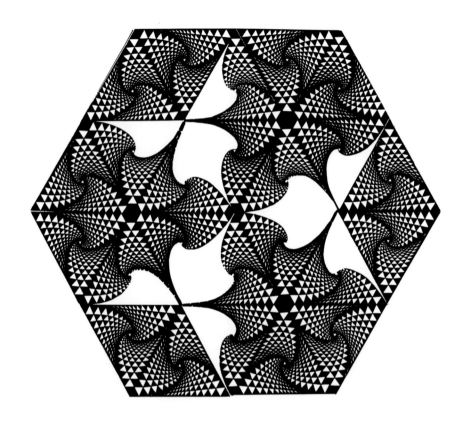

GRAZIOTTI

One of the 108 drawings of variations on Adriano Graziotti's flat triangular modular composition, 1975.

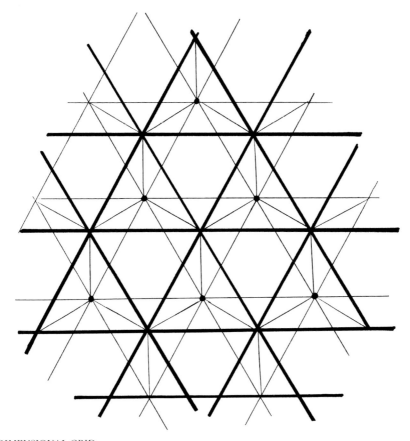

THREE-DIMENSIONAL GRID

The grid is composed of two overlapping planes of equilateral triangular structures. The top grid, marked in a darker colour, is shifted in relation to the underlying grid, lighter coloured, so that, when lying flat, the intersecting bars forming the structure are in the middle of the triangles below, marked by a dot. The distance between the two planes is given by the connecting bars which join the intersecting top bars to the centres of the bottom triangles. The bars connecting the two planes are also marked in a lighter colour and are the same size as the sides of the triangles.

This is the most solid three-dimensional grid that can be constructed to form a bearing plane.

GREY

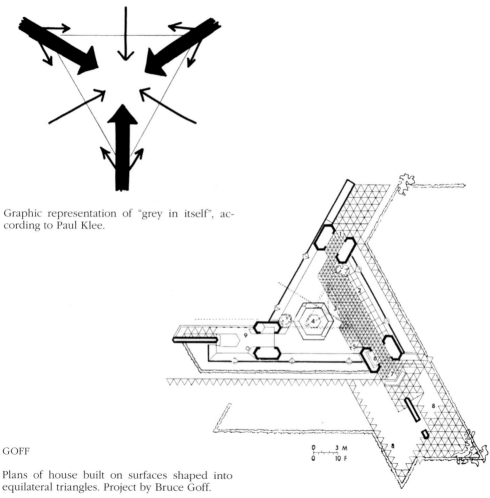

Graphic representation of "grey in itself", according to Paul Klee.

GOFF

Plans of house built on surfaces shaped into equilateral triangles. Project by Bruce Goff.

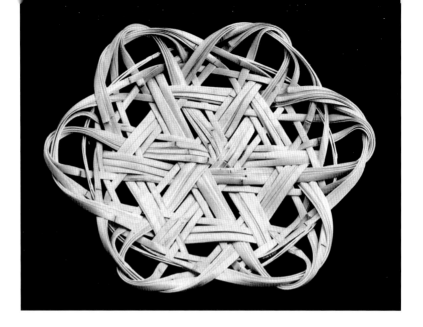

WEAVE

Weave of triangular-structured bamboo. Japanese craftsmanship.

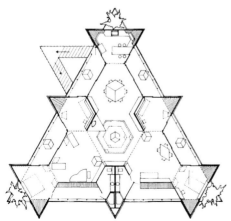

HYDRODICTYON

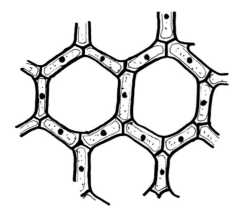

Reticular structure of a *Hydrodictyon reticulatum*.

ICOSAHEDRON

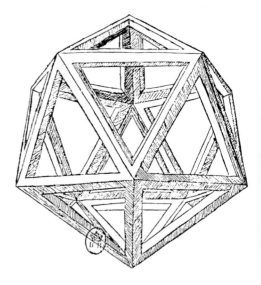

Sculptural form designed by Leonardo.

HITTITES

The sign for a city and for a king in Hittite writing.

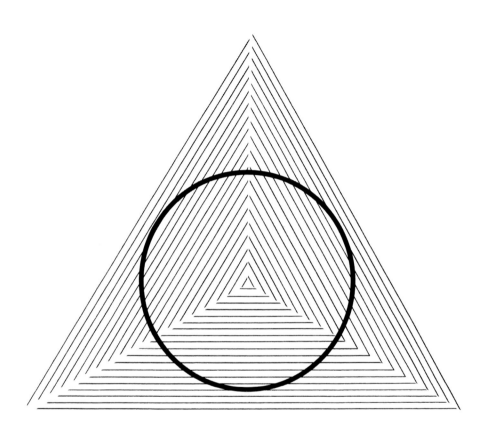

OPTICAL ILLUSION

A circle drawn on an expanding triangular surface is not perceived as a perfect circle but actually appears to be deformed.

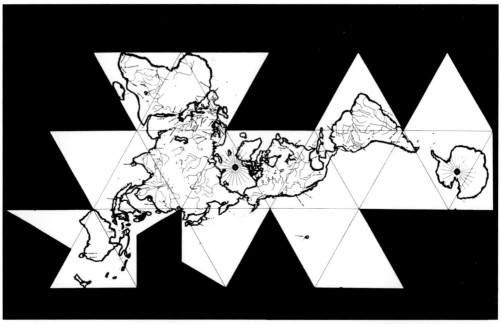

ATLAS

New way of showing the continents based on an idea by Buckminster Fuller, 1934.

LE CORBUSIER

Diagram of three human settlements by Le Corbusier, 1947. The linear industrial city ideally takes up one side of the triangle, the other two sides are formed by the radiocentric exchange city, the farm settlement unit is in the centre.

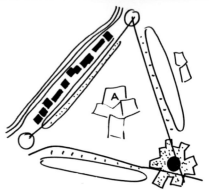

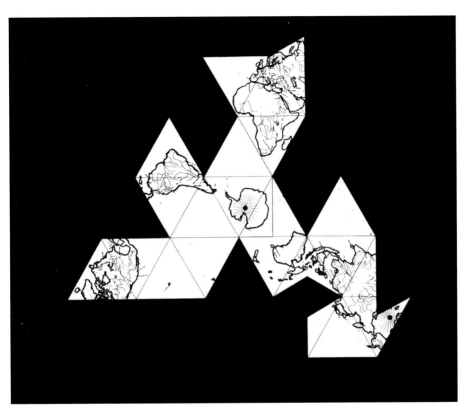

MOUNTAIN

Old Chinese sign for a mountain.

MACROSPORE

Germinating macrospore.

METEOROLOGY

Meteorological symbols standing for: stormy sky, snowstorm, storm, hail.

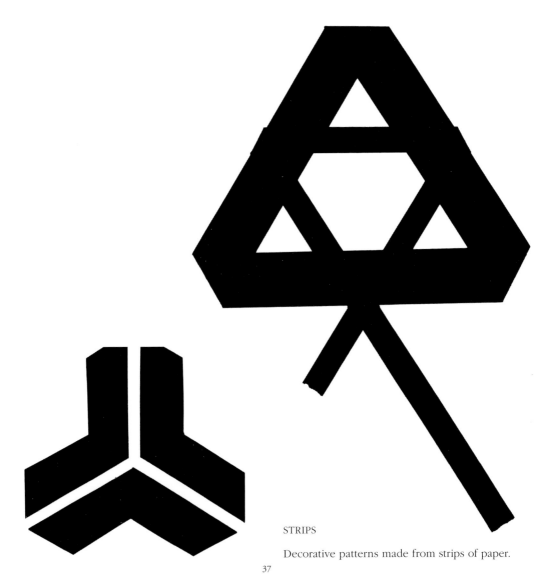

STRIPS

Decorative patterns made from strips of paper.

MERCEDES

Logo designed by Gottlieb Daimler.

LOGO

Logo for a car rally organised by Italian Television, designed by Giancarlo Iliprandi.

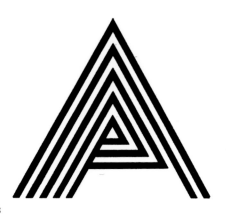

LOGO

Designed by Marcel Wyss.

LOGO

Designed by Eugen and Max Lenz.

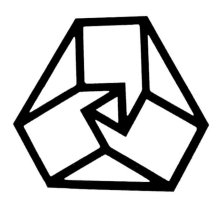

LOGO

Designed by Yusaku Kamekura.

LOGO

Idea for a logo.

LOGO

Idea for a logo.

LOGO

Designed by Russel A. Sandgren.

LOGO

Designed by Tom Geismar.

LOGO

Designed by Ilio Negri.

LOGO

Designed by Altes Familienzeichen.

LOGO

Designed by Neukomm and Pinschewer.

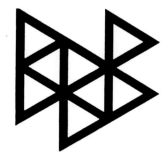

LOGO

Designed by Hans Hartmann.

LOGO

Idea for a logo.

ENGINE

Wankel rotating engine driven by a triangular piston. During the first phase, side A shuts off the discharge and intake ports. B is where compression takes place and C hosts the expansion phase. During the second phase induction begins in A, B completes compression and C starts the discharge. During the third phase A continues the induction, B begins to start up and C continues with the discharge. During the fourth phase induction is completed in A, B starts up the expansion phase, while discharge continues in C.

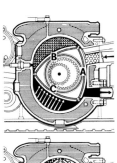

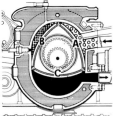

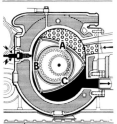

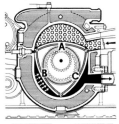

MESSAGE

Message sign.

 INDUCTION   COMPRESSION   WORKING STROKE   EMISSION

NANNUCCI

Variation on an equilateral triangle by Maurizio Nannucci, 1970.

ORIGIN

Triangular signs from which the alphabet originates.

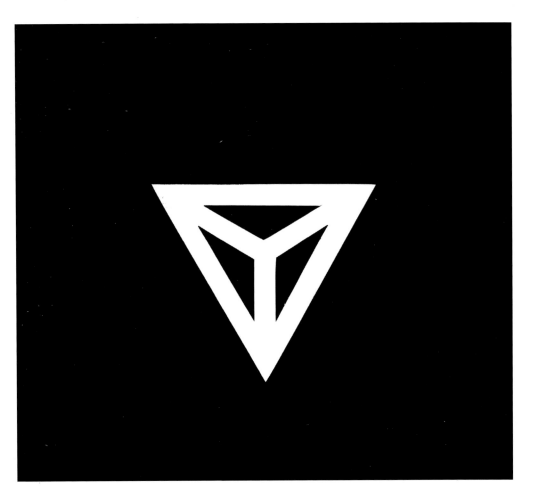

DRAGON'S EYE

Ancient oriental symbol.

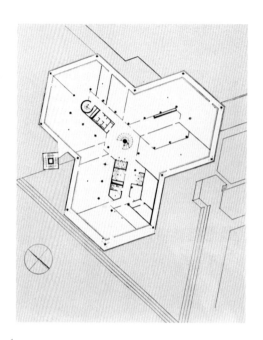

NIZZOLI AND OLIVERI

Plan of the ENI buildings in San Donato Milanese.

TRIANGULAR NUMBERS

Series of numbers arranged into a triangular pyramid as if they were spheres. The triangular numbers are, for example: 1 3 6 10 15 21 28...

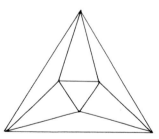

OCTAHEDRON

Octahedron set out on a plane according to the "geometry of a rubber sheet".

FLOOR

Old floor made of hexagonal tiles, each divided into three different colours. The overall effect is of ambiguous relief.

PERÙ

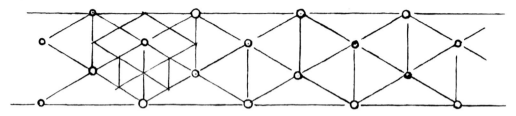

Structural diagrams of ancient Peruvian decorations.

POLLEN

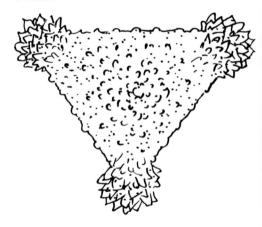

Grains of Proteaceae pollen.

PETROGLYPHS

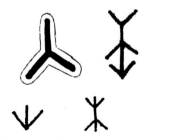

Prehistoric rock engravings. Inyo – California.

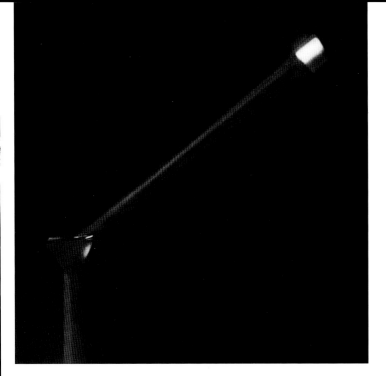

PRISM

"In 1666, the year when I set about cutting optical glass into non-spherical forms, I prepared a triangular prism in order to experiment into the famous colour phenomena. To this end, having made my room dark and cut a hole in the window to let a convenient amount of sunlight in, I placed my prism where it flowed in, so that it would be refracted onto the opposite wall. It was a real joy for me to study the bright, intense colours this produced". So Newton described his discovery.

PUNIC

Ancient Punic symbol of the cult which worshipped the goddess Tanit-Astarte.

PLANKTON

PERRY

Two sculptures by Charles O. Perry, created by rotating and combining together triangular elements, 1964.

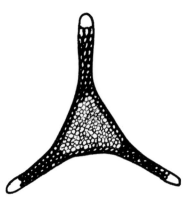

One of the forms of plankton elements.

PARDI

Studies into shapes that can be obtained from an equilateral triangle based on its measurements and using only a ruler and compass.
Gianfranco Pardi, 1970.

THEREFORE

Three points arranged into a triangle in mathematical language stands for: therefore.

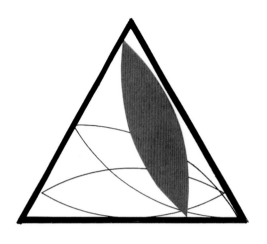

INTERNAL ROTATION

A lens-shaped form, generated from two symmetrical curves whose radius is the apothem of an equilateral triangle, can rotate inside the triangle itself, always touching the sides.

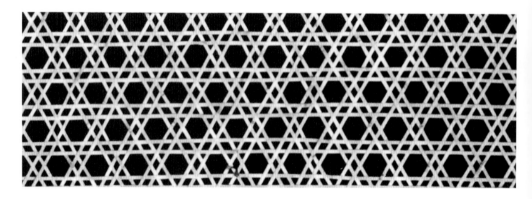

GRID

One of the most popular grids in the works of Japanese bamboo craftsmen.

PAVILIONS

Exhibition pavilions with a truncated tetrahedron built for the Montreal Expo, 1967.

FOUR ELEMENTS

The symbols of fire, air, water and earth, symbols of Medieval alchemy.

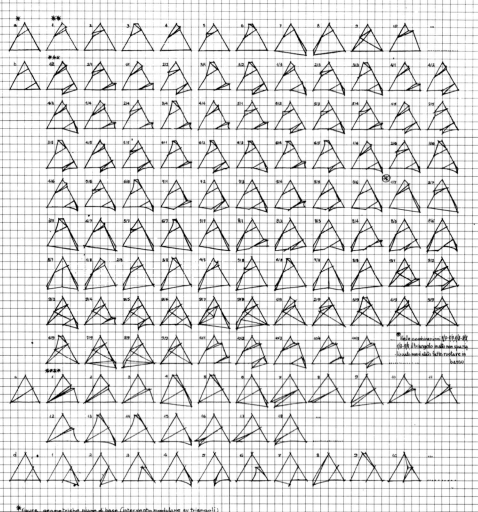

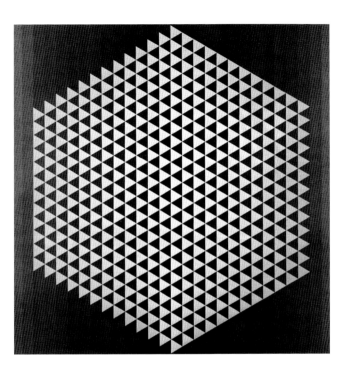

RISARI

Chromatic cross fading on a triangular structure in a painting by Piero Risari, ESA-12, 1974.

ROTTA LORIA

Studies into the spatial relations of an equilateral triangle by Claudio Rotta Loria.

RUST

Two symbols of Medieval alchemy standing for rust.

ROTATION EXPANSION

Rotation and expansion of a triangle, drawing by Franco Grignani.

RUNIC

Runic symbols for man, woman, procreation, pregnancy, family, friendship, quarrel, the death of a man and death of a woman.

ROAD SIGNS

Signs for a campsite, water supply and school.

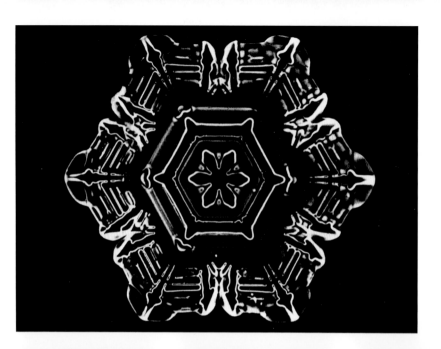

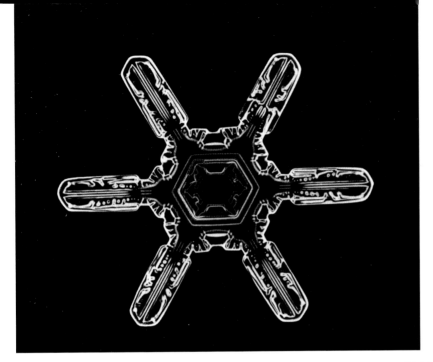

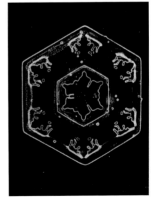

SNOWFLAKES

The photographs of snowflakes show how many variations nature creates while keeping strictly within a triangular and hence hexagonal framework.

INTERNAL STRUCTURE

One of the possible internal structures of a tetrahedron as a module for intricate constructions.

BEGGARS' SIGNS

The first means danger, the second drinking water.

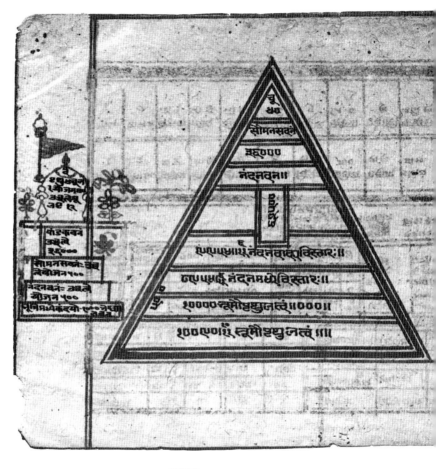

SHIVA

The triangle stands for matter in the visual symbols of the Tantra cult. If its tip is pointing upwards it is the symbol for Shiva.

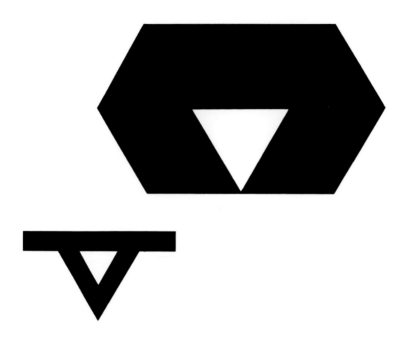
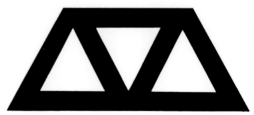

SAMBONET

Symbols for some of the signs of the Zodiac designed by Roberto Sambonet. They are the symbols for Taurus, Aires and Libra.

FOLDING CHAIR

This chair, made of wood and leather, can be folded away leaving the three legs held together by the strap.

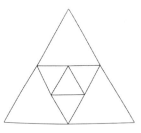

SCARPA

Triangular object with even-sized folding internal triangles that can be transformed into other shapes. The object was designed and made by Giorgio Scarpa out of metal tubes and nylon threads that holds them all together and allows them to fold.

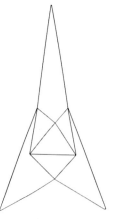

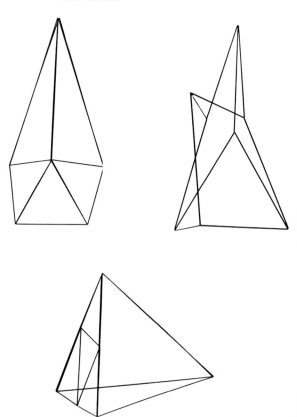

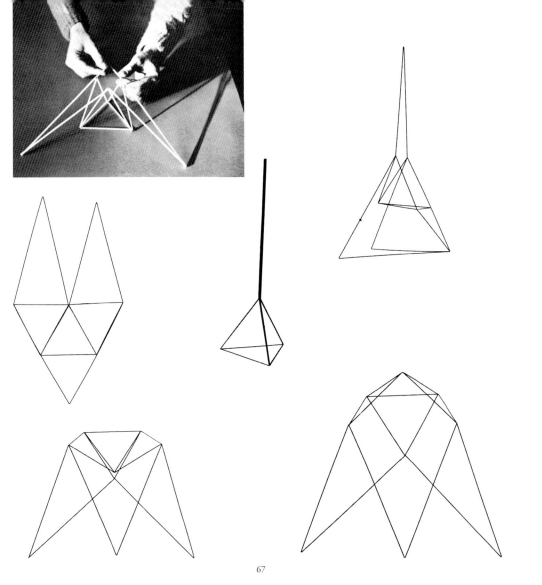

SCARPA

Tetrahedron divided into eight parts joined together to make them adjustable. The object, designed by Giorgio Scarpa, can be transformed into lots of other unexpected shapes.

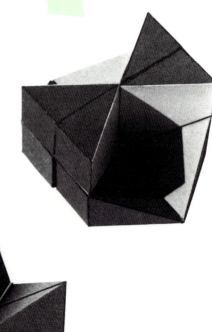

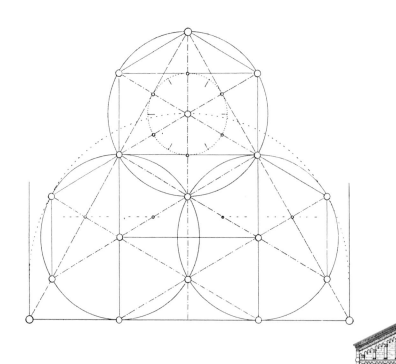

SAN ZENO

Drawing of the façade of San Zeno Church in Verona and a diagram of its harmonious structural layout. From a study by Ernst Mössel.

SIX CURVED FACES

Six square surfaces joined together by overlapping the corners form a sort of curved-faced cube with triangular gaps visible between the surfaces.

EARTH

Medieval symbol for the earth.

JAPANESE COATS-OF-ARMS

All Japanese families have a coat-of-arms representing their craft/commercial trade or just identifying them. These coats-of-arms always have very precise designs based on simple forms and their internal measurements. The following pages show some triangular-structured coats-of-arms.

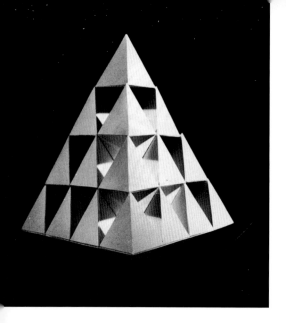

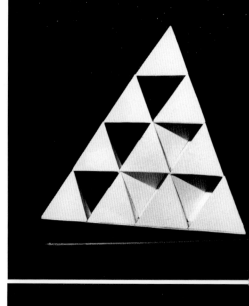

EXPERIMENTATION

Example of the modularity of the tetrahedron and its negative and positive variables. Student: Thais Padron, Caracas.

Arrangement of tetrahedrons in space showing the internal pathways. Student: Kokonen Kaarina, Finland.

Structural genesis of the equilateral triangle. Student: Claude Dubois, Paris.

Teacher: Prof. Carlo Nangeroni. School: Milan Design Polytechnic.

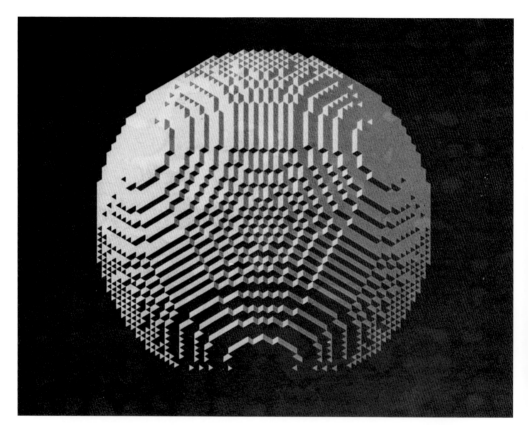

EXPERIMENTATION

Appearance of triangular organisation in the transformation cycle of a cube full of tiny cubes inside a sphere. The operation takes place by removing the same number of tiny cubes from each side in the same order. Jan Slotuber and William Graatsma.

TERRACOTTA

Marking on old terracotta works.

EXPERIMENTATION

Modulated forms in the two-dimensional triangular structure, which can be read both negatively and positively. Each of these forms may be combined with other similar forms touching in accordance with the rules of rotational symmetry or translation. Student: Giuseppina Marchetti. Milan Design Polytechnic, teacher: Bruno Munari, 1973.

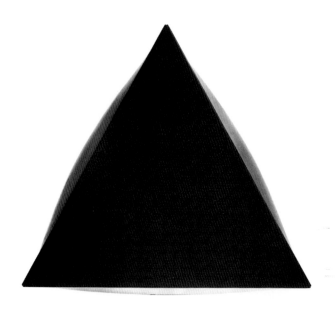

TELEVISION SET

Triangular-based television set designed by Mario and Dario Bellini, allowing components to be assembled in a minimum space and making the appliance more adaptable to its setting.

STONECUTTERS

Personal symbols of stonecutters from the Romanesque period.

TRIPOD

Three-legged objects are always steady even on uneven surfaces. They may wobble if they have four legs. So tripods and camera-stands for photographers or cameramen or for precision instruments for making optical observations always have three legs the same distance from each other.

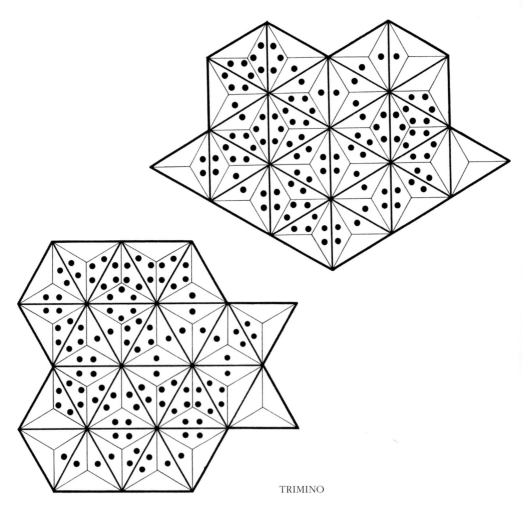

TRIMINO

A game with the same rules as dominos but with triangular-shaped pieces which can be combined in different ways.

SPHERICAL TRIANGLE

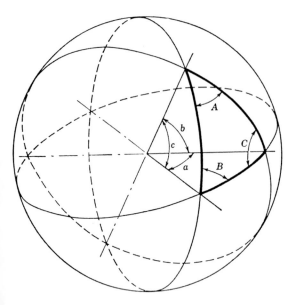

This is a triangle constructed on the surface of a sphere. Any side of any spherical triangle is a segment of circumference whose radius is the radius of the sphere, so the tips of a spherical triangle are always an intersection between the radius of the sphere and the surface, so any side of a spherical triangle may be expressed by means of the angle formed by the two radiuses determining the tips corresponding to the side in question. The properties of spherical triangles are: each angle of a spherical triangle is, by definition, always less than 180 degrees. The sum of the angles determining the sides is somewhere between 0-360 degrees and the sum of the angles of the triangle is between 180-540 degrees.

TRINACRIA

Ancient symbol of Sicily on an old coin.

CURVED TRIANGLES

MUSICAL TRIANGLE

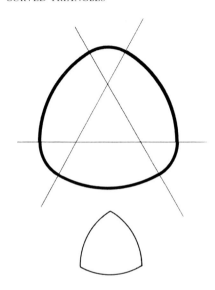

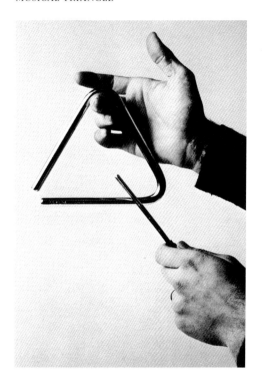

The curves are obtained from arcs of a circle whose centre is at the tip of the triangle.

TRI-RECTANGULAR TRIANGLE

A spherical triangle whose three angles are all right-angles.

TERRESTRIAL TRIANGLE

A spherical triangle constructed on the earth's surface, taken in this case as a sphere, whose tips are one of the poles and any other two points.

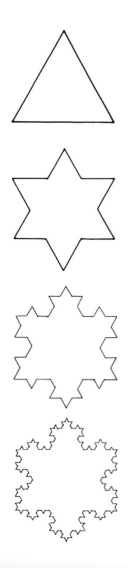

GRADUAL TRANSFORMATION

Gradual transformation of a triangle into a snowflake shape, constantly repeating the same operation of dividing up the sides and growing towards the outside of the figure.

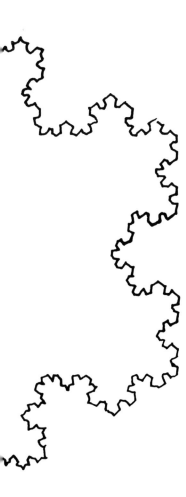

POLAR TRIANGLE

A spherical triangle constructed inside a given spherical triangle, joining together the poles of the various sides (i.e. the point along the side closest to the opposite tip of the triangle).

IMPOSSIBLE TRIANGLE

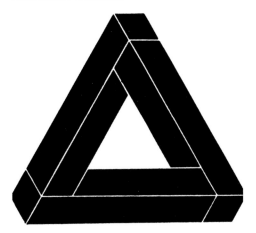

Triangular form which can be described on a plane but is impossible to construct in three dimensions. Invented by L. S. Penrose.

REFRACTORY TRIANGLES

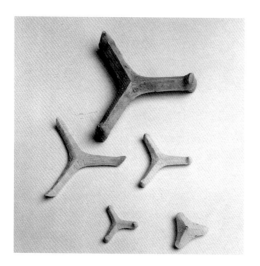

Rests with three equidistant support points used for firing ceramics to keep the objects being baked separate from each other.

TETRAPAK

Plastic-coated milk carton obtained from a cylinder by sealing the two circular apertures above and below with two linear seals at right-angles to each other.

MAGIC TRIANGLE

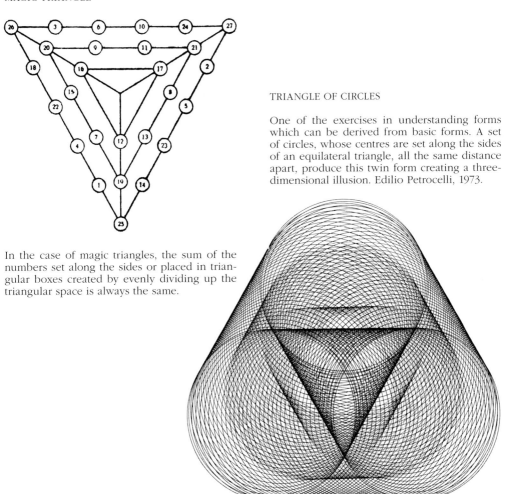

In the case of magic triangles, the sum of the numbers set along the sides or placed in triangular boxes created by evenly dividing up the triangular space is always the same.

TRIANGLE OF CIRCLES

One of the exercises in understanding forms which can be derived from basic forms. A set of circles, whose centres are set along the sides of an equilateral triangle, all the same distance apart, produce this twin form creating a three-dimensional illusion. Edilio Petrocelli, 1973.

TOVAGLIA

A logo and two triangular-based patterns by Pino Tovaglia, 1975.

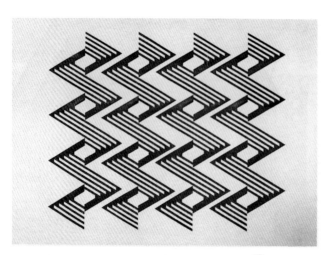

TOMSHINSKY

Psycho-technical mosaic game designed by Tomshinsky, 1968. The triangular elements in the six colours of the spectrum can be combined on hexagonal surfaces. The personality of the player is revealed by the choice of colours and how they are set out within the hexagon.

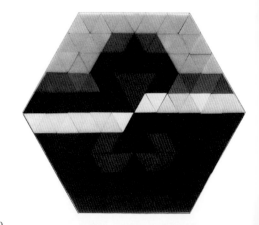

ARMED MAN

Sign used by beggars to indicate the presence of somebody carrying a weapon.

EQUAL AREA

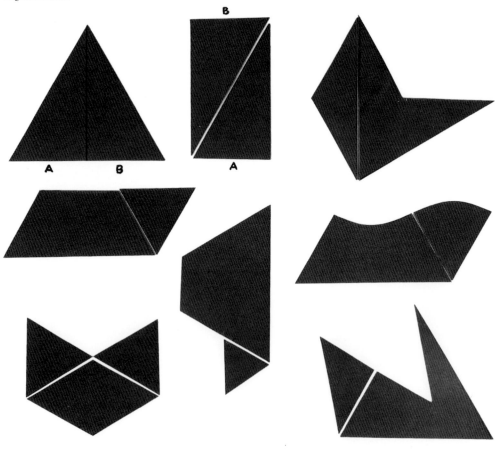

Transformation of a triangular surface into other forms with the same area by inventing rules for breaking down and recomposing the figure.

TRAY

Bamboo tray constructed around a hexagonal weave.

VALLÉ

Six angular triangles. Wooden sculpture painted by Thea Vallé.

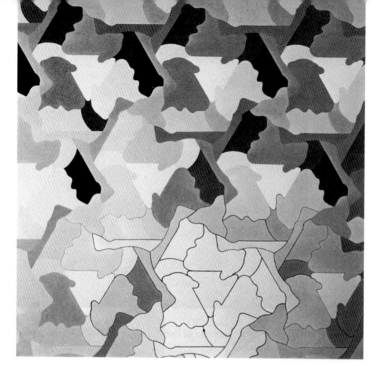

WOODMAN

Acrylic paint on canvas. The forms are produced by deforming a triangular web. George Woodman, 1971.

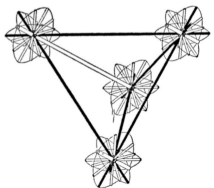

WACHSMANN

Joint design for a steel structure. Konrad Wachsmann.

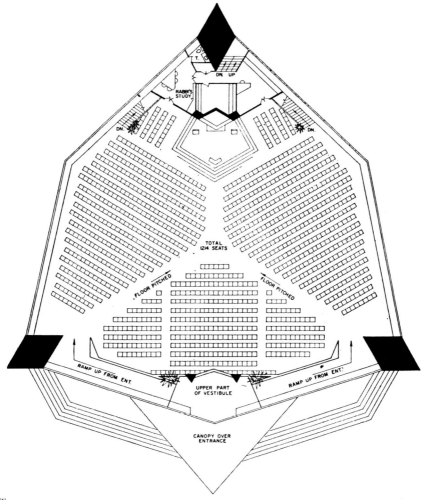

WRIGHT

Plan of the House of Peace built in Elkins Park and designed by Frank Lloyd Wright in 1959.

YOGA

The perfect position tends to create an equilateral triangle shape with your body. This is done as follows: 1 sit on the ground with your legs extended; 2 fold your left leg by placing your foot on the inside of your thigh; 3 fold your right leg and place your foot over your left leg slipping the tip of your foot in the gap between your calf and thigh. Your right heel should be pressing against the pubic bone, both knees should be firmly touching the ground; 4 place the palm of your right hand on your right knee and the palm of your left hand on your left knee; 5 sit up straight but not stiffly keeping your head and back perfectly straight.

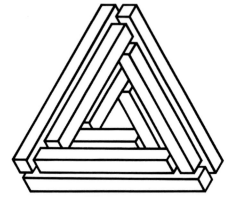

YTURRALDE

A drawing and painting of impossible figures.
J. M. Yturralde, 1968-1971.

YTURRALDE

Drawings in search of impossible figures.
J. M. Yturralde, 1971.

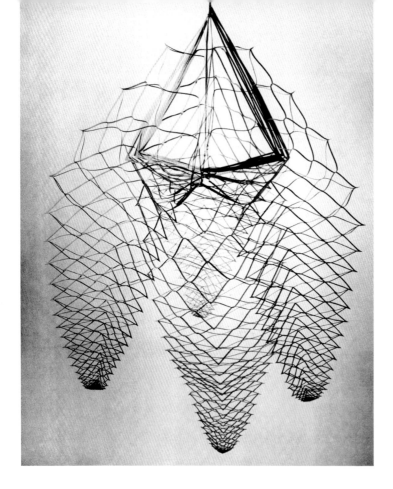

ZALEWSKI

Transformation of a cardboard triangle into a three-dimensional object by making cuts in accordance with the internal measurements of the triangle. Joseph Zalewski, 1953.

SULPHUR

Symbol for sulphur.

EDWIN A. ABBOTT

Flatland is an imaginary tale of a two-dimensional world inhabited by segments, triangles, squares and miscellaneous polygons. The women in this country are Segments, the soldiers and workers from the lower classes are Isosceles Triangles with very short bases. The middle classes are Equilateral Triangles, the professionals and gentlemen are Squares or Pentagons. The aristocracy is composed of all the figures with more than five sides forming a hierarchy within the hierarchy and, finally, the high class of priests is composed of Circles. In this two-dimensional world a Square has the vision or rather perception of a sphere and finds it very hard to be believed by his fellow inhabitants.

The symbolic use of geometric forms obviously creates a scale of social values, so it is interesting to read how the author describes the birth of an equilateral triangle belonging to the family of isosceles triangles (of a lower rank):

"Rarely – in proportion to the vast numbers of Isosceles births – is a genuine and certifiable Equal-Sided Triangle produced from Isosceles parents. Such a birth requires, as its antecedents, not only a series of carefully arranged intermarriages, but also a long-continued exercise of frugality and self-control on the part of the would-be ancestors of the coming Equilateral, and a patient, systematic, and continuous development of the Isosceles intellect through many generations.

The birth of a True Equilateral Triangle from Isosceles parents is the subject of rejoicing in our country for many furlongs round. After a strict examination conducted by the Sanitary and Social Board, the infant, if certified as Regular, is with solemn ceremonial admitted into the class of Equilaterals. He is then immediately taken from his proud yet sorrowing parents and adopted by some childless Equilateral, who is bound by oath never to permit the child henceforth to enter his former home or so much as to look upon his relations again, for fear lest the freshly developed organism may, by force of unconscious imitation, fall back again into his hereditary level".

E. A. Abbott, *Flatland*, Bibliotaca Adelphi, 7, Milan 1966.

MIKHAIL ZOSHCHENKO

In his collection of *Moscow Tales* Mikhail Zoshchenko describes *The Terrible Night* of Boris Ivanovic' Kotoféjev, a triangle player in a symphony orchestra prey to his own sad thoughts.
"Of course the reader will sometimes have seen the man with a rather sagging jaw at the back of the orchestra, over on the right, bent over his little iron triangle. What is he doing? He sadly runs his fingers back and forth over his simple percussion instrument. The conductor generally follows him with a watchful eye, the right one. Boris Ivanovic' Kotoféjev lived in a little wooden house painted yellow, together with Lukeria Petrovna. Nothing very eventful had ever happened in his life, everything just rolled along smoothly and quietly. Then one day Boris suddenly found himself thinking that everything changes in life, that you cannot take anything for granted and that if modern technology resulted in the invention an electric musical triangle that played itself, then he Boris Ivanovic' would be out of a job. "And if I give up playing the triangle how could I carry on living? It is all that keeps me alive", he told his wife one day, but she consoled him: "Then I will have you on my back, you son of a dog".
That wonderful bright and clear summer evening, Boris was walking along the streets gesticulating nervously, he drank a glass of beer at the station, carried on walking without knowing where to go, entered the cemetery and exclaimed: "Calligraphy today, drawing tomorrow, that is the way life goes!" He lit a cigarette, "I will get by somehow", he thought. He tried begging, with no success. A group of bystanders stopped, Boris started to run off. He hid in church, ran up the bell tower with the people following him. He reached the bells: he rang them with all his might until they carried him away.
But the next day, all perfectly neat and tidy as always, he sat down in the orchestra and nothing in his expression gave away the terrible night he had just gone through".

M. Zoshchenko, *Moscow Tales*, Longanesi, Milan 1951.

Sources of the illustrations

pg. 92: Richard H. Althoff.
pg. 22-23: Photo Ugo Mulas. Copyright © Eredi Ugo Mulas. All rights reserved.
pg. 56-57: Carl Zeiss, Oberkochen.
pg. 9: from *Forme giapponesi*, D. Richie and A. N. Nii. Photographs by Takeji Iwamiya. Silvana Editoriale d'Arte, Milan 1963.
pg. 59: photographs by Alberto Munari.
pg. 69 (c): from *Cubic Construction Compendium 1970*, Cubic Construction Centre, Heerlen, The Netherlands.

INDEX

As all the subjects in this book have been arranged in alphabetical order (as far as make-up allows) no index is necessary.

THE TRIANGLE
DISCOVERY OF THE TRIANGLE
Bruno Munari

© 1976 Bruno Munari
All rights reserved by Maurizio Corraini s.r.l.
No part of this book may be reproduced or transmitted in any
form or by any means (electronic or mechanical, including
photocopying, recording or any information retrieval system)
without permission in writing from the publisher.

Original first edition published in 1976 Zanichelli, Bologna
Maurizio Corraini first edition 2007, in a new format
The publisher will be at complete disposal to whom might be related
to the unidentified sources printed in this book.

Translation by Martyn John Anderson

Printed in Italy by Grafiche SiZ, Verona July 2007

Maurizio Corraini s.r.l.
Via Ippolito Nievo, 7/A
46100 Mantova
Tel. 0039 0376 322753
Fax 0039 0376 365566
e-mail: sito@corraini.com
www.corraini.com